In Celebration of

_____

_____

Date

_____

Guest Name
(address/phone #/email)

Notes

_____

_____

_____

_____

_____

_____

_____

_____

_____

_____

_____

_____

_____

Guest Name
(address/phone #/email)

Notes

_____

_____

_____

_____

_____

_____

_____

_____

_____

_____

_____

Guest Name
(address/phone #/email)

Notes

_____

_____

_____

_____

_____

_____

_____

_____

_____

_____

_____

_____

Guest Name
(address/phone #/email)

Notes

_____

_____

_____

_____

_____

_____

_____

_____

_____

_____

_____

_____

Guest Name
(address/phone #/email)

Notes

Guest Name
(address/phone #/email)

Notes

Guest Name
(address/phone #/email)

Notes

Guest Name
(address/phone #/email)

Notes

Guest Name
(address/phone #/email)

Notes

Guest Name
(address/phone #/email)

Notes

_____

_____

_____

_____

_____

_____

_____

_____

_____

_____

_____

_____

Guest Name
(address/phone #/email)

Notes

Guest Name
(address/phone #/email)

Notes

_____

_____

_____

_____

_____

_____

_____

_____

_____

_____

_____

Guest Name
(address/phone #/email)

Notes

_____

_____

_____

_____

_____

_____

_____

_____

_____

_____

_____

_____

_____

Guest Name
(address/phone #/email)

Notes

_____

_____

_____

_____

_____

_____

_____

_____

_____

_____

_____

_____

_____

Guest Name
(address/phone #/email)

Notes

_____

_____

_____

_____

_____

_____

_____

_____

_____

_____

_____

_____

_____

Guest Name
(address/phone #/email)

Notes

_____

_____

_____

_____

_____

_____

_____

_____

_____

_____

_____

_____

_____

_____

Guest Name
(address/phone #/email)

Notes

Guest Name
(address/phone #/email)

Notes

_____

_____

_____

_____

_____

_____

_____

_____

_____

_____

_____

_____

_____

_____

Guest Name
(address/phone #/email)

Notes

_____

_____

_____

_____

_____

_____

_____

_____

_____

_____

_____

_____

_____

Guest Name
(address/phone #/email)

Notes

Guest Name
(address/phone #/email)

Notes

_____

_____

_____

_____

_____

_____

_____

_____

_____

_____

_____

Guest Name
(address/phone #/email)

Notes

_____

_____

_____

_____

Guest Name
(address/phone #/email)

Notes

Guest Name
(address/phone #/email)

Notes

Guest Name
(address/phone #/email)

Notes

Guest Name
(address/phone #/email)

Notes

_____

_____

_____

_____

_____

_____

_____

_____

_____

_____

_____

_____

_____

_____

Guest Name
(address/phone #/email)

Notes

_____

_____

_____

_____

Guest Name
(address/phone #/email)

Notes

_____

_____

_____

_____

_____

_____

_____

_____

_____

_____

_____

_____

_____

_____

Guest Name
(address/phone #/email)

Notes

Guest Name
(address/phone #/email)

Notes

_____

_____

_____

_____

_____

_____

_____

_____

_____

_____

_____

_____

Guest Name
(address/phone #/email)

Notes

_____

_____

_____

_____

_____

_____

_____

_____

_____

_____

_____

_____

_____

_____

_____

Guest Name
(address/phone #/email)

Notes

Guest Name
(address/phone #/email)

Notes

_____

_____

_____

_____

_____

_____

_____

_____

_____

_____

_____

_____

_____

Guest Name
(address/phone #/email)

Notes

Guest Name
(address/phone #/email)

Notes

Guest Name
(address/phone #/email)

Notes

_____

_____

_____

_____

_____

_____

_____

_____

_____

_____

_____

_____

_____

_____

Guest Name
(address/phone #/email)

Notes

_____

_____

_____

_____

_____

_____

_____

_____

_____

_____

_____

_____

_____

Guest Name
(address/phone #/email)

Notes

_____

_____

_____

_____

_____

_____

_____

_____

_____

_____

_____

_____

_____

_____

Guest Name
(address/phone #/email)

Notes

Guest Name
(address/phone #/email)

Notes

_____

_____

_____

Guest Name
(address/phone #/email)

Notes

_____

_____

_____

_____

_____

_____

_____

_____

_____

_____

_____

_____

_____

_____

_____

Guest Name
(address/phone #/email)

Notes

Guest Name
(address/phone #/email)

Notes

_____

_____

_____

_____

_____

_____

_____

_____

_____

_____

_____

_____

_____

Guest Name
(address/phone #/email)

Notes

_____

_____

_____

_____

_____

_____

_____

_____

_____

_____

_____

Guest Name
(address/phone #/email)

Notes

_____

_____

_____

_____

Guest Name
(address/phone #/email)

Notes

_____

_____

_____

_____

_____

_____

_____

_____

_____

_____

_____

_____

Guest Name
(address/phone #/email)

Notes

_____

_____

_____

_____

_____

_____

_____

_____

_____

_____

_____

_____

_____

Guest Name
(address/phone #/email)

Notes

_____

_____

_____

_____

Guest Name
(address/phone #/email)

Notes

_____

_____

_____

_____

_____

_____

_____

_____

_____

_____

_____

_____

_____

Guest Name

(address/phone #/email)

Notes

_____

_____

_____

_____

_____

_____

_____

_____

_____

_____

_____

_____

_____

_____

Guest Name
(address/phone #/email)

Notes

Guest Name
(address/phone #/email)

Notes

Guest Name
(address/phone #/email)

Notes

_____

_____

_____

_____

_____

_____

_____

_____

_____

_____

_____

_____

_____

_____

_____

Guest Name
(address/phone #/email)

Notes

_____

_____

_____

_____

Guest Name
(address/phone #/email)

Notes

Guest Name
(address/phone #/email)

Notes

_____

_____

_____

_____

_____

_____

_____

_____

_____

_____

Guest Name
(address/phone #/email)

Notes

Guest Name
(address/phone #/email)

Notes

_____

_____

_____

_____

_____

_____

_____

_____

_____

_____

_____

_____

_____

Guest Name
(address/phone #/email)

Notes

Guest Name
(address/phone #/email)

Notes

_____

_____

_____

_____

_____

_____

_____

_____

_____

_____

_____

_____

_____

_____

Guest Name
(address/phone #/email)

Notes

_____

_____

_____

_____

_____

_____

_____

_____

_____

_____

_____

_____

_____

Guest Name
(address/phone #/email)

Notes

Guest Name
(address/phone #/email)

Notes

_____

_____

_____

_____

_____

_____

_____

_____

_____

_____

_____

_____

_____

Guest Name
(address/phone #/email)

Notes

_____

_____

_____

_____

_____

_____

_____

_____

_____

_____

_____

_____

_____

Guest Name
(address/phone #/email)

Notes

Guest Name
(address/phone #/email)

Notes

Guest Name

(address/phone #/email)

Notes

_____

_____

_____

_____

_____

_____

_____

_____

_____

_____

_____

_____

_____

_____

Guest Name
(address/phone #/email)

Notes

Guest Name
(address/phone #/email)

Notes

_____

_____

_____

_____

Guest Name
(address/phone #/email)

Notes

_____

_____

_____

_____

_____

_____

_____

_____

_____

_____

_____

_____

_____

Guest Name
(address/phone #/email)

Notes

Guest Name
(address/phone #/email)

Notes

_____

_____

_____

_____

_____

_____

_____

_____

_____

_____

_____

_____

_____

_____

Guest Name
(address/phone #/email)

Notes

_____

_____

_____

_____

_____

_____

_____

_____

_____

_____

_____

_____

Guest Name
(address/phone #/email)

Notes

_____

_____

_____

_____

_____

_____

_____

_____

_____

_____

_____

_____

_____

_____

_____

Guest Name
(address/phone #/email)

Notes

_____

_____

_____

_____

_____

_____

_____

_____

_____

_____

_____

_____

_____

Guest Name
(address/phone #/email)

Notes

_____

_____

_____

_____

Guest Name
(address/phone #/email)

Notes

_____

_____

_____

_____

Guest Name
(address/phone #/email)

Notes

_____

_____

_____

_____

_____

_____

_____

_____

_____

_____

_____

_____

_____

_____

Guest Name
(address/phone #/email)

Notes

Guest Name
(address/phone #/email)

Notes

_____

_____

_____

_____

_____

_____

_____

_____

_____

_____

_____

_____

Guest Name
(address/phone #/email)

Notes

Guest Name
(address/phone #/email)

Notes

Guest Name
(address/phone #/email)

Notes

Guest Name
(address/phone #/email)

Notes

_____

_____

_____

_____

_____

_____

_____

_____

_____

_____

_____

_____

Guest Name
(address/phone #/email)

Notes

_____

_____

_____

_____

_____

_____

_____

_____

_____

_____

_____

_____

Guest Name
(address/phone #/email)

Notes

Guest Name
(address/phone #/email)

Notes

_____

_____

_____

_____

_____

_____

_____

_____

_____

_____

_____

_____

_____

Guest Name
(address/phone #/email)

Notes

Guest Name
(address/phone #/email)

Notes

Guest Name
(address/phone #/email)

Notes

_____

_____

_____

_____

_____

_____

_____

_____

_____

_____

_____

_____

_____

Guest Name
(address/phone #/email)

Notes

_____

_____

_____

_____

_____

_____

_____

_____

_____

_____

_____

_____

Guest Name
(address/phone #/email)

Notes

_____

_____

_____

_____

_____

_____

_____

_____

_____

_____

_____

_____

_____

_____

Guest Name
(address/phone #/email)

Notes

_____

_____

_____

_____

_____

_____

_____

_____

_____

_____

_____

_____

_____

_____

Guest Name
(address/phone #/email)

Notes

Guest Name
(address/phone #/email)

Notes

Guest Name
(address/phone #/email)

Notes

_____

_____

_____

_____

_____

_____

_____

_____

_____

_____

_____

_____

_____

Guest Name
(address/phone #/email)

Notes

_____

_____

_____

_____

_____

_____

_____

_____

_____

_____

_____

_____

_____

Guest Name
(address/phone #/email)

Notes

_____

_____

_____

_____

_____

_____

_____

_____

_____

_____

_____

_____

_____

_____

Guest Name
(address/phone #/email)

Notes

Guest Name
(address/phone #/email)

Notes

_____

_____

_____

_____

_____

_____

_____

_____

_____

_____

_____

_____

Guest Name
(address/phone #/email)

Notes

Guest Name
(address/phone #/email)

Notes

Guest Name
(address/phone #/email)

Notes

_____

_____

_____

_____

Guest Name
(address/phone #/email)

Notes

_____

_____

_____

_____

_____

_____

_____

_____

_____

_____

_____

_____

_____

_____

Guest Name
(address/phone #/email)

Notes

Guest Name
(address/phone #/email)

Notes

Guest Name
(address/phone #/email)

Notes

Guest Name
(address/phone #/email)

Notes

Guest Name
(address/phone #/email)

Notes

Guest Name
(address/phone #/email)

Notes

_____

_____

_____

_____

Guest Name
(address/phone #/email)

Notes

Made in United States
Orlando, FL
05 May 2022

17527429R00065